Harry Ramsden

The Uncrowned King of Fish-and-Chips

Don Mosey & Harry Ramsden Junior

DALESMAN
Publishing Company Ltd

The Dalesman Publishing Company Ltd.
Clapham, via Lancaster, LA2 8EB
This edition 1994
First published 1989

© Text, Don Mosey
© Illustrations, Harry Ramsden Junior

ISBN : 1 85568 088 2

The publishers gratefully acknowledge the support and co-operation
of Merryweathers Ltd in the production of this book.
The "Harry Ramsden" signature on the cover and title page
is the copyright of Harry Ramsden's (Restaurant) Ltd
and is reproduced with their kind permission.

PRINTED BY B. R. HUBBARD LTD, SHEFFIELD

Contents

Prologue

THIS is not so much the family history of a renowned Yorkshireman as an expression of love and admiration by a son for his father. Harry Ramsden III had read a hundred articles in praise of his Dad but still, at the age of 65, longed to see those tributes more formally expressed and in greater detail. With two cousins, Lewis junior and Edith, he painstakingly gathered anecdotes and reminiscences from other relatives, from friends and from business associates; without their researches and the material they gathered, this book could not have been written.

Why, you may well ask, does it now come to be put together by a cricket commentator whose previous authorship has been about that game, about golf and about travel? The answer is simple. Yorkshire CCC used to be the greatest cricket club in the world; West Riding fish and chips are the best in the world and the man who spread their fame most effectively to the four corners of the earth was Harry Ramsden.

After a lifetime's love affair with Yorkshire cricket and with fish and chips, what is wrong with combining the best of both words?

- D.M.

Opposite: **Harry Ramsden - uncrowned king of fish-and-chips.**

This photograph of Annie Ramsden's wedding shows Grandfather Harry seated at the right. Also in the picture are (left to right) Harriet Ramsden; Harold France; Annie; and Harry Ramsden.

Grandfather Harry Ramsden

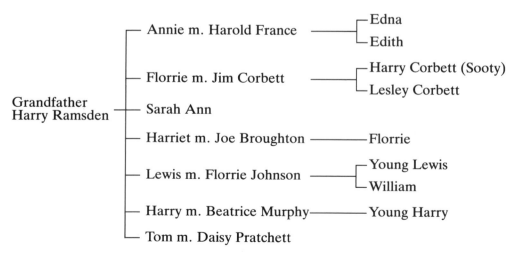

Grandfather Harry was the founder of the Ramsden fish-and-chip empire at No. 22 Manchester Road, Bradford. His eldest child, Annie, married Harold

Left: **Harry Ramsden with his sister Sarah Ann;** *right:* **Annie Ramsden.**

France, a fire engine driver who was decorated for his rescue work after the Low Moor munitions explosion. Her brother Harry was chauffeur *and* best man at the wedding. Edith is the daughter of Harold and Annie France. Florrie, who promised to keep house for and "look after" her father as long as he lived (and she did so), afterwards married Jim Corbett. Their son, Harry, was the man who gave to the entertainment world the much-loved glove puppet, Sooty – bought on the North Pier at Blackpool during a family holiday there.

Grandfather Harry's brother, Charlie, was a tram-driver on the Manchester Road route. There are no prizes for guessing where he took his meals. His daughter, Elsie, married Albert Cowling, founder of those great West Riding bars which, pre-war, advertised: "A pork pie, a half-pint, a cigarette, a box of matches – and you'll still get change from sixpence." Albert Cowling's wine lodges pioneered the sale of wine by the glass long before anyone dreamed of taking holidays in Spain.

Early Days

OUR story really begins with the man we must call Grandfather Harry since our cast of characters includes three principals with the name of Harry Ramsden. The supporting cast is made up of men – and women – who would have been entirely at home in a J.B. Priestley play of his earlier years, men like Jimmy Jackson, Billy Robinson, Harry Sugden, not forgetting Mrs. Ineson, the queen of cleaning ladies. In its way, the Ramsden story reflects the social history of the West Riding in the first half of this century – a tale of poverty, bad housing and its natural consequence, ill-health; of cheeky humour and risky enterprise; of Yorkshire personalities richly-endowed with characteristic stubbornness and sheer bloody-mindedness. And as an epilogue we have the words of Harry III, "young" Harry, uttered in a voice choked with a mixture of love, admiration, pride and awe as he delivered the final verdict on The Uncrowned King of Fish and Chips: "What a man... what a man to have as your Dad".

The dynasty was founded by Grandfather Harry, sometime stage-door manager, publican and policeman, a bit of a rough diamond, who opened his fish-and-chip shop at 22 Manchester Road, one of Bradford's humbler working-class districts, around the turn of the century. He had seven children – four daughters, Annie, Florrie, Sarah Ann and Harriet – followed by three sons – Lewis, Harry and Tom. It was the most modest beginning imaginable to an empire which was to become, quite literally, world-renowned. There was a single frying range at 22 Manchester Road, coal-fired; preparation of both fish and chips was carried out without a single electronic aid of any kind in the beginning and Grandfather Harry did not even own the lease of his premises. When, after his death, the lease was bought over the heads of his heirs and successors (Lewis and Florrie) and they were given notice to quit, they were offered just four pounds for the fixtures and fittings, "providing they threw in a dynamo" which had been acquired to drive the potato-cleaning rotary.

Old Harry, with rough Victorian paternalism, believed firmly in the work-ethic as a cardinal priciple of bringing up his family. All the children, as they grew

Manchester Road, Bradford, in 1911. In the background is Grandfather Harry's fish-and-chip shop; fish was then a penny and chips a halfpenny!

to adulthood, were expected to help in the shop: chopping chips, filleting fish, lighting the coal fires, frying and serving. We see the first touch of *the* Harry Ramsden's individuality in his refusal to join his brothers and sisters in any of these duties. His father, from the photographs which exist of him, does not look the type of man to take filial rebellion lightly and it must have taken a good deal of courage for Harry to go his own way. But he did. We see him first getting up at 4 a.m. to start work in Ambler's mill at 5 a.m., going to school part-time and doing an evening stint as lather-boy in a barber's shop. There is something graphically Dickensian about it all as there is indeed about his subsequent success-story.

9

He had a spell as a telegram delivery boy and alternated with re-packaging parcels which had come adrift. Next he worked for a taxi firm and before he was into his twenties we find him running two cabs of his own. How can he possibly have got together the capital to do that? By borrowing – and here we have our first glimpse of the sheer daring of the man, but to appreciate it the occasion has to be seen in context. No bank on earth would have loaned money to this young man without an asset to his name. It had to be done privately and that meant moving into a jungle of deadly danger. There were working-class families in the early part of the 20th century who never, throughout their entire lives, got clear of debts and indeed who passed them on to their children. It was a desperately risky business to go to the Edwardian equivalent of loan-sharks with their exorbitant rates of interest. What Harry had to do was find a private individual with a bit o' brass to spare who wanted a decent return on his capital. He was astute (or fortunate) enough to do this and immediately established as the first principle of his business life: "Always pay your debts when they are due". And he never again, throughout all his trading, experienced difficulty in getting a loan. Everyone knew that Harry Ramsden always repaid loans and did so without equivocation or delay.

By the time he was 21, the taxicab business had lost its appeal and he decided to become a publican. The lease of the Craven Heifer in Bolton Road, Bradford, was available and he approached, first, his father for a loan to pay for the fixtures and stock valued at £68 0s 6d. Grandfather Harry greeted the request cynically: "I'll lend thee enough to see a doctor to 'ave thi' 'ead examined... thinkin' o' takin' a pub at 21!"

The reaction had no doubt been anticipated. Harry addressed himself to H. Walker & Co. Ltd., 28 Barry Street, Bradford, and borrowed £73 to be repaid at 30s a week, beginning on 3rd July, 1911. "Young" Harry delves into the family archives and produces the faded red repayments book showing £1 10s paid regularly, on the dot. Along with it comes a notebook, detailing in the immaculate copperplate hand of Arthur Beckett, Licensed Valuer, the transfer of the pub from Richard Haley to Harry Ramsden: "One 48-inch mahogany bound bar, three iron-framed tables, upright pianoforte in walnut by R.H. Deighton and Co, London, two fire-bricks, three round stools, three iron spitoons, 19 glass-handled pints, three glass-handled half-pints, three mould goblets, five tots, 13 mould tumblers,

Opposite: **Two of Harry Ramsden's taxi cabs. He is driving the one shown in the upper photograph, while brother Lewis has taken the wheel in the lower picture.**

The Craven Heifer Hotel in Bolton Road, Bradford, in 1911. Harry Ramsden took the tenancy in that year when he was only twenty-one.

21 pint pots stamped…" Nothing was too insignificant to excape the professional eye of Mr. Beckett: "*Part* set of dominoes, coal-saver, poker and ashtray."

All the new landlord needed now was customers and that was clearly not going to be easy. The Craven Heifer was badly run down with virtually no "regulars" at all. H.R., however, noticed that a neighbouring establishment was doing a lively trade and decided that a reconnaisance was necessary. The secret of his rival's success, he discovered, was a pianist. The good folk of Bolton Road liked a good tune with their ale and so they had music every evening except Sunday. Well, there was no problem about that. Harry arranged a meeting with the pianist, offered him double the money he was being paid and got himself some live music. But when he applied for a music licence to the magistrates it was refused! Stalemate? Not a bit of it. Harry went ahead with his musical evenings, posting a look-out at the door of his pub. At the first sign of the approach of The Law, the watcher pressed a button which rang an alarm-bell inside the Craven Heifer and musical entertainment was temporarily suspended.

It was an uphill battle. He was "open" from six in the morning and when the first family members called one evening to see him Harry had sold one pint of beer all day! The pianist changed that – or at any rate the pianist brought the customers in in the first place and Harry's gift for showmanship and salesmanship did the rest. It started out as a challenge. He had been told from the first that the Craven Heifer was "a bad spec". It had had one landlord after another and none of them had been able to make a living in the place. All that meant to Harry Ramsden was that he had to find a way of *making* it pay. He did not believe that there was any business venture *he* could not make successful and he proved his point over the years – with one exception, as we shall see, but that was 20 years in the future. The set-back he now encountered was one which no one could do anything about – the First World War.

Off he went to serve as an Army transport driver, notably in the Salonika campaign where his brother Tom also fought. They never met each other until, coming home on leave, they both got off the same train at Forster Square Station and, with astonished delight, greeted each other before turning to their sister Sarah Ann who was on the platform to meet them.

Harry did not return to the licensed trade after the war. But he and his wife Beatrice set up home at 2 Southbrook Terrace near the bottom of Great Horton Lane where Beatrice (Beaty) provided theatrical digs for stars of the variety stage playing at the Palace and Alhambra Theatres and also "put up" footballers who played for the two clubs in the city. Harry had now, at last, gone into the fish-and-chip trade, first with a lock-up shop at Wibsey Fair, then on to more familiar family territory at the corner of Manchester Road and Bower Street, which was open every lunchtime, every tea-time and every night on 365 days a year! Even at Christmas? *Especially* at Christmas. And when relatives questioned the wisdom of such a step Harry's reply was couched in terms of devastating logic: "Don't *you* get bloody fed up of turkey?" And while it is doubtful if too many working-class families in the 1920s could enjoy a large turkey at Christmas, even those in the most straitened circumstances contrived some sort of seasonal fare, if only for the sake of the children. Simple economics made it

Left: **Harry Ramsden at Salonika during the 1914/18 war;** *above:* **Mobile billboard for Harry's shop in Westgate, Bradford – ninepence would buy fish, chips, tea, bread and butter.**

Opposite: **Forerunner of great things to come – the wooden, lock-up fish-and-chip shop at White Cross, Guiseley, which Harry Ramsden bought for £150 in 1928. The upper photograph dates from about that time; the lower one from the 1950s.**

necessary to eke out the festive board over several days and there can be no doubt that somewhere to buy fish-and-chips at that time of the year would be popular. The shop prospered and more staff were taken on – girls who came from the even-more-depressed areas like County Durham, along with Jimmy Jackson, a teenage barrow-boy from Seven Dials who **walked** from London to West Yorkshire in 1923 and was to become one of Harry's most valued and trusted retainers.

Next came a second shop, in Westgate, and then Harry bought the clothing shop next door and turned it into the Cosy Café with black and white tiles and hunting prints around the walls, decor which was to become his trade-mark. The theatrical lodgings run by Beatrice now began to play their part in the expansion of Harry's business. Comedians playing the theatres introduced, woven into their patter, a reference to having been to Harry Ramsden's for fish and chips and those members of the audience who had not up to that point heard of the Cosy Café were tempted to go in search of it. It was wonderful free advertising and Harry was on to a winner.

There was only one cloud on the horizon during the next five years but sadly it was a major one. The birth of "young" Harry in 1924 had left Beatrice virtually an invalid. She suffered from tuberculosis which was a scourge of those times and with no drugs to combat it the generally-accepted treatment was a long period of convalescence in conditions of clean, fresh air. Indeed, a sanatorium was built high on the moors above Grassington which housed many patients from Bradford, and during my own childhood, nine miles away in Keighley. I remember many of my consumptive school friends going off to what was known as "the open air school" at Braithwaite, one of the highest points on the hills surrounding that huddle of factory chimneys down in the Worth Valley. Some recovered; many didn't.

Harry Ramsden now embarked on his own method of making life easier for his ailing wife and their frail, sickly son who was afflicted by a weak chest throughout his childhood. In December 1928 he withdrew £150 from his bank account and bought a wooden, lock-up fish-and-chip shop in Otley Road, White Cross, and moved Beatrice and young Harry into a cottage beside the White Cross public house. It did not work. Sadly, Beatrice died in 1929. She had not time to see the 200-seater restaurant her husband built almost directly across the road from their cottage. She never enjoyed life in Larwood House, the home that Harry built and named to express his admiration for the Notts. and England fast bowler after the Bodyline Tour to Australia of 1932-33. She died before his name had given first, respectability, to fish-and-chips as a dining-out meal and then opulence to the setting in which the dish was dispensed. She never rode in his Lea Francis car or took a Mediterranean cruise with him. But one likes to think she had a good idea of the success that was to be his.

White Cross

TO appreciate the ambitious nature of the Harry Ramsden restaurant at White Cross when it was opened in 1931 it is necessary to take a close look at the working class community of the West Riding at that time. It was only five years after the General Strike; the severe industrial crisis which overwhelmed Britain as a whole and resulted in the formation of the National Government had created chronic unemployment. There was little, if any, modern housing development and the great woollen mills of the Bradford area (on short-time working weeks) were surrounded by acres of streets of two-up, two-down terraced houses, usually without bathrooms and with outside toilet facilities. In my own home, the income (represented by my father's wage in the combing department of a Keighley mill) was 30 shillings a week, or £1.50 in modern currency. This was supplemented by a few shillings for collecting outstanding debts from a doctor's "panel" patients and a modest honorarium for Dad's services as a football club groundsman and similar seasonal duties for a cricket club. We would be a fairly typical working-class family of the period. A modest joint of meat was somehow contrived at the week-end by my mother, a house-keeping genius, and it was made to last three days in one form or another (e.g. meat-and-potato pie was Monday's main meal) and Friday was always fish-and-chip day. With my small brother, not two years old in 1931, not yet involved in the meal, two fish for my parents, a scone (as it was called in Keighley, fish-cake in Bradford) for me, and one portion of chips shared by the three of us, it meant that an entire family meal could be provided for less than one shilling (5p). So naturally enough, small fish-and-chip shops flourished on just about every street corner of industrial West Yorkshire; they were an essential part of our society.

They were utilitarian operations, like Grandfather Harry's business in Manchester Road – a single, coal or coke-fired range frying fish for twopence or threepence, cakes (scones) at 1½d or 2d, and chips at a penny (the earliest prices I personally remember). The phrase "a fish and a penn'orth" is still part of my vocabulary – and one remembered wth great affection and relish, too.

17

Fish-and-chip shops with small cafés attached to them where customers could sit at a table and have tea and bread and butter as well were regarded as a bit posh and a meal in that sort of establishment was a rare "treat". Children's weekly pocket-money was usually pitched at the "Saturday penny" level and how to spend it was for so many years the major financial problem of my young life. A penny would buy two ounces of boiled sweets, pay the return fare into the town centre, purchase anything up to a half pound of broken biscuits at Marks and Spencers, admit one to the swimming baths or to a Saturday morning matinee at the cinema. If one chose to "split" the penny, then it was still possible to have a one-way bus-trip into or out of Keighley and to buy "a ha'porth of scraps" at the fish shop. Scraps were (still are, happily, available) the spare bits of batter which had become detached from the frying fish and which the proprietor scooped out from time to time to deposit in a corner of the range. Fried a deep brown, with salt and vinegar applied, they were delicious.

This, then, was the world geared to extreme frugality into which Harry Ramsden launched his great restaurant at the beginning of the 1930s. Just what his vision of the future was, it is difficult to determine. There seemed no end in prospect to the poverty the country had known for years. Ownership of a car was beyond the wildest imaginings of the sort of customers he had served in Manchester Road and in Westgate or Wibsey while White Cross was not the sort of urban development he could expect to see transformed into a mass population area. How could the visionary Mr. Ramsden have seen so clearly and so shrewdly into the next two or three decades? How could he possibly have visualised a time when so many families would either own, or have access to, a car of their own? And how could he have foreseen that people owning their own homes, cars, TV sets and the other trappings of modern affluence would then *still* retain their affection for the humble fish-and-chip lunch, tea or supper?

It is difficult to find any clue to his picture of the future, either from his family, his friends or his business associates. What does emerge, however, is a very clear impression of a man who believed that you must never stand still; that, however gloomy the prospects, you must always be looking ahead, seeking improvements, not just keeping pace with progress but anticipating it. Initially, he looked for his custom amongst the working-class people he understood and with whom he identified.

The working man (and woman) would provide the bulk of his trade and his first concentration was on the out-sales – the takeaway side of his business at

Washed and peeled potatoes, ready for cutting into chips, were stored in huge wooden tubs. Moving these to the chipping machine was a cumbersome job, so Harry Ramsden designed a metal base on casters.

White Cross. The restaurant was for the future and he would watch its progress with interest but to finance that part of the venture he had to be sure of bulk sales in the shop. It started with a price-war waged against a neighbouring café which he won because he had adequate financing and because he could always find a man to back him with additional money it he needed it.

His attention to detail in trading was just as effective. While the small street-corner fish shops worked on a by-guess-or-by-God basis (or, in the case of the more meticulous proprietors, by applying long experience), Harry applied slide-rule techniques. He had long since established the principle that if the temperature of the hot fat in his frying-range was correct "there was no chip ever cut by man which could not be cooked to perfection in three minutes". With his fish, frying time was five minutes but there was more to it than that…

"You would not think," recalls his son, Harry junior, "that you can fry a piece of fish the wrong way up. But you can. Dad absolutely insisted that the battered piece should be dropped into the fat with the side from which the skin had been cut facing upwards. Then, after 2½ minutes exactly it had to be turned over and fried for another 2½ minutes. The result was the perfect fried fish."

There was more – much more. Washed and peeled potatoes, ready for cutting into chips, were stored in huge wooden tubs – in water, of course – and these were cumbersome loads to move between the washer and the chipping machine. It was a two-man job, and time-consuming as well. Harry designed a metal base, on casters, for the tubs to rest on so that a small child could propel them about the shop. But once again we see no detail escaping the master: every morning one of the duties of the odd-job man was *to oil* the casters.

He had thermometers cut into the frying pans and no chips could be put into the fat until its temperature registered 350 degrees. He had stainless steel buckets specially made which took exactly the correct measure of chips to be cooked at one time. Every frier carried a small metal six inch ruler for checking the level of the cooking fat (dripping) which had to be never less than 3½ inches so that all frying was carried out at the same temperature. If the level dropped, the temperature changed. His ranges were custom-built by Frank Fords, of Halifax, whose representative, one Tommy Jones, visited White Cross to ask what his specific requirements were.

And so to the batter, for so long a vital factor in achieving the supremacy of Yorkshire fish-and-chips. Every shop with any sort of reputation has always insisted on keeping its recipe for batter a closely-guarded secret. In all the best products, the quality of the batter is just as important as the quality of the fish, and of the chips. Harry Ramsden's ingredients were measured with an excruciating care, even down to a specially-made measure for adding precisely the required amount of water to the 3lb and 6lb bags of batter-mix. The scales were checked every day and if any measure of any ingredient was "out" by as much as one grain, great was the wrath of Ramsden senior. He even installed an electrically-powered mixer designed for the bakery trade, rather than using one made specifically for the fish-frying industry, arguing that if precision was essential in confectionery,

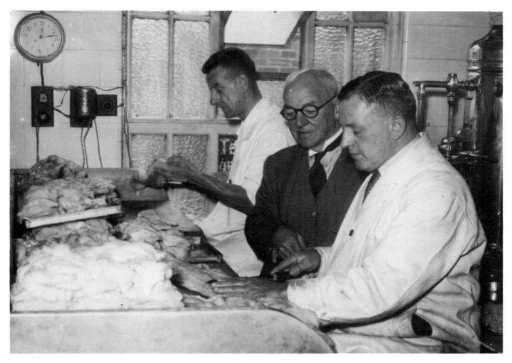

Fish preparation in progress. Harry Ramsden – the ultimate perfectionist – had the benches fitted with stainless steel tops so that scrubbing of the wooden surfaces could be eliminated.

it was no less so in batter-preparation.

His fish-preparation benches were mady by his own joiner, Horace Nelson, and it did not take Harry long to spot the amount of time which had to be spent at the end of the day scrubbing the dense wooden surfaces to clear out lingering scraps of fish which worked their way into minute cracks and cuts. Back he went to the tinsmith in Rawdon (who had created to Harry's design the mobile bases for the potato-tubs) and a stainless steel top was fitted to the preparation benches. At the end of the day it could be hosed down in minutes and another time-and-labour-saving procedure had been introduced. Next came movable scrays, or wooden platforms, for the friers to stand on as they supervised the pans. Even in the best-regulated premises a certain amount of spillage of liquid fat on to the tiled floor was inevitable and when it congealed a dangerous skating-rink type of surface resulted underfoot which required a great deal of cleaning. The scrays could be taken up at the end of the day, carried outside and scrubbed with boiling water and caustic soda. More time saved.

And so we see, as a fish-frier and restaurateur, Harry Ramsden was the ultimate perfectionist, believing first and foremost in absolute cleanliness, making sure that every corner of his premises was spotless before the day's business began and in a similar state before they closed for the night.

"He was," recalls his son, "more interested in the state of the dustbins than the contents of the tills." The bins had to be properly covered at all times and emptied regularly. Any that showed the slightest sign of over-flowing before the binmen arrived had to be removed and replaced. He would not tolerate any employee with long and untidy hair. "Would *you* like to be served with food of any sort by a chap with hair hanging over his collar?" he demanded. He religiously checked the condition and the quality of fish *and* chips as they were sold and his niece, Edith, saw him – not once, but frequently – throw away chips which were "too brown", an indication that they had been overcooked.

To make sure that he was completely au fait with *everything* in his shops and restaurants, Harry prepared a list of daily tasks which he, as the proprietor (or one of his staff duly delegated), had to carry out. The list had 100 items! It was pinned to the back of a cupboard door and Harry never left until every single job had been carried out and ticked off from the list. It covered everything from ensuring there was an adequate supply of flour for batter-making to his all-consuming pre-occupation with cleanliness. This was a fetish with him. He searched high and low for a cleaner he could trust to regard proper hygiene with the same religious zeal as he observed himself. At last he found this paragon, a Mrs. Ineson, and as he triumphantly announced the end of his exhaustive search to young Harry he carried out a small demonstration. "Watch this," he instructed, dropping a match on to the floor. "She won't miss it." And it was a small victory for him as Mrs. Ineson came into view, duly spotted the match and whisked it into her dustpan. Harry oozed with satisfaction. "I told thee," he beamed delightedly.

He offered a reward of a pound for any practical ideas from the staff which would improve efficiency and "young" Harry designed a sieve with a special scraper for use when the pans were given their regular scouring. It earned him a fiver – far more than a week's wages in the shop – for "a damned good idea". Harry confesses, "I probably got five times the usual reward because I was the son – but it was certainly worth a quid".

So much for the behind-the-scenes operations. Let us now look at the restaurant which was years ahead of its time when it was first opened. Genius though he undoubtedly was, Harry Ramsden nevertheless soon found that he couldn't "win 'em all". He was proud of his cutlery, with each knife, fork and spoon bearing his name but it did not take long to realise that the very exclusivity of it made him vulnerable. The cutlery began to disappear at an alarming rate as customers took away souvenirs of their first visit to the world's biggest fish-and-chip shop. No Yorkshireman, let alone businessman, could tolerate that and Harry quickly reverted to simple anonymity in his knives, forks and spoons. The tea came in the usual stainless steel pots, with a separate one for hot water to top up the teapot. Now, at one time or another I suppose everyone who has used metal teapots anywhere in the world has been infuriated by the inevitability of spillage. No matter how much care is exercised in pouring the tea, nothing is more certain than that a certain amount will miss the cup and trickle down the front of the pot on to the tablecloth and even on to the food if one is unwary enough to hold the cup over the top of it! Harry was having none of that. He brought in a team of experts to devise teapots which would not drip. (I wonder what happened to them because all over the world I have found that teapots still drip.)

The original floor was of rubberoid tiles and quickly Harry found that even in the best-regulated restaurant waitresses very occasionally spilled an odd chip from the heaped plates. Nowadays the proprietor's concern would be at the possibility of being sued by a customer who happened to slip on an accidentally discarded chip; in the less litigation-conscious 1930s, when fewer people could afford even to contemplate a visit to a solicitor let alone begin an action for damages, it was simply a matter of proprietorial pride that the risk be eliminated. Wall-to-wall carpeting was introduced.

Lighting was tasteful without being pretentious, with chandeliers over the tables enhancing the wall-brackets – not the *crystal* chandeliers which were introduced, post-1954 by Eddie Stokes when he managed the business – but still immensely avant garde in a 1930s fish 'oil. And the leaded lights in the windows evoked one reaction of childish innocence which immediately became part of the folklore of Harry Ramsden's. The cashier heard a small boy, who looked round in wonderment while his father was paying his bill, ask: "Dad, is this where God comes for his fish and chips?" It is a remark which tells us two things about Life more than half a century ago – first that the child had never seen anything like the restaurant at White Cross; secondly that he was not unfamiliar with the interior of a church, or at least a Sunday School.

At the opposite end of the restaurant from the entrance was a raised area on which discreet entertainment was provided from time to time by a pianist – often Harry Corbett – for Harry Ramsden was a great believer in unobtrusive music to accompany a wholesome meal. Long before supermarkets had been conceived and only the more salubrious hotels had introduced music, Harry was on to it. He even had firm ideas on what was the *right kind* of music – Charlie Kunz tinkling away on his piano in his immediately-recognisable style – and before long-playing records had been devised he had a set of eight of those heavy, 78 r.p.m. discs loaded on to apparatus in his office and the music piped, pianissimo, into the restaurant.

From the childhood and teenage memories of son Harry jnr we get, amidst all this opulence, a glimpse of his father as the archetypal "tight" Yorkshireman who loved the idea of making pennies while the pounds could take care of themselves, and, in parallel, one who absolutely hated losing a penny needlessly. "He installed little slot machines on the wall," Harry recalls, "which cost a penny to play and you whirled a steel ball round and round. If it ended up in one of the five slots in the centre, you got your money back and a free go; if it went into either of the other two slots, you lost. My Dad used to stand and watch and every time a punter lost he was overjoyed. He watched them for hours and he damn near hugged himself. On the other hand, nothing enraged him more than to lose a penny on the immaculate new toilets he installed. They worked on a penny-in-the-slot basis – the door would only open if an "old" penny was inserted – and, human nature being what it is, a lot of people used to leave without closing the door properly so that the next 'customer' could find it ajar and save a penny. This, of course, meant my Dad had *lost* a penny and it infuriated him so he had the locks taken off and a turnstile installed so that nobody could get into a toilet for nothing!"

At the same time, those toilets were always spotless and the soap in the washroom area was changed three and four times a day. Harry's dictum was: "If you want to know what a restaurant is really like, inspect the toilets before you go in to eat. If that end of things is clean, you can enjoy your meal there; if it is "rough" then you are simply seeing a facade and you can bet the hygiene in the kitchen will be no better than that in the washrooms." It is a philosophy which is as true today as it was in 1931.

Having done everything he felt was necessary for the restaurant customers and the outsales to factories or to eat at home, Harry now began to think about the people who bought their fish-and-chips to eat on the spot. At one side of his

As part of the policy of providing everything possible for the restaurant customers, two snooker tables were installed in the basement at Harry Ramsden's. This photograph shows the star snooker and billiards player, Willie Smith.

premises was a long dividing wall which separated him from a couple of semi-detached houses and he now called up the busy joiner, Horace Nelson, once again, to build a long bench-seat against the wall. Next came a dozen or so small tables with salt and vinegar available so that the "out-patients" could sit and eat their meal there. But what if it was raining? No problem. Harry brought in another contractor to put a roof over this alcove. This then created a problem with the wind which whistled through, blowing papers all over the place and quickly cooled the lunch, tea or supper of those who were not quick eaters. Again, it was a challenge to be faced and Harry dealt with it by having the end of the sit-down area blocked off with glass panels and swing doors placed in position: end of draughts and windswept meals. And still he hadn't finished. A window was now cut into the kitchen wall and through this a girl served cups of tea and the meal was complete. For the price of *takeaway* fish-and-chips, the customer could now sit down and eat in relative comfort if not the luxury of the restaurant-proper.

His attention to detail may be seen again in the meticulous care he took to ensure that his clock, at the front of the restaurant, was checked daily. It was a distinctive time-piece with the figures on the face replaced by the twelve letters which make up the name "Harry Ramsden". It was used by conscientious bus drivers (and their inspectors in the days when such things mattered) to check the time that buses passed the restaurant. It was a West Yorkshire company driver who told "young" Harry: "There's only two public clocks in the country that you can always rely on. One's Big Ben and t'other's Harry Ramsden's". And Harry made sure that this was always so. He would check two and three times a day and if his clock was out by so much as a minute a man was despatched up to the roof to correct it.

It has to be said that some of his researches in pursuit of the ideal take one's breath away. Take, for instance, the vinegar bottles... at a chemist's shop in Guiseley, Harry bought a bottle of liquid used – a few drops at a time – to add to water in which dentures were soaked overnight. "That's it," he announced delightedly, much as Archimedes must have gloated at his discovery that the water-level in his bath rose in direct ratio to his bodyweight. "That's the right amount of vinegar needed to season a fish and a penn'orth." And he went back to the chemist to ask, "How many bottles of this 'ere stuff to the case?"

"Two dozen," replied the chemist. "Right," said Harry, "I want five cases."

Then there was the matter of the vinegar itself... Harry, in his never-ending search for ultimate perfection, felt his mushy peas were not *quite* as tasty as some he had tried. He consulted Pie Herbert, another legendary Bradford purveyor of simple, cheap, toothsome snacks: pork pie swimming in a dish of peas, seasoned to the customer's personal specifications with salt, pepper and vinegar.

"Why are your peas tastier than mine?" inquired Harry, with blithe disregard for the fact that he was probing into a trade secret.

"They're not," replied Herbert, professional delight overcoming business discretion. "It's t'vinegar that's different." He then disclosed that instead of buying ready-to-use bottles of processed vinegar he bought the "real stuff" in bulk and filled his own bottles from a cask.

Away went Harry to Grimshaws of Leeds with an order for casks of "neat" vinegar and another item was added to his list of (at least) 100 daily tasks to be performed before he opened for the day: vinegar bottles to be filled from the cask. He hated the sight of bottles on his table with the last few drops of vinegar covering the bottom. One member of his staff had to check every morning and any bottle which was less than half-full had to be replenished.

Still the search for perfection was not complete. Lewis Grimshaw, on a monthly call at the restaurant, noticed a "mould" forming in a vinegar bottle –

a natural process with the pure malt variety – and, feeling this might be a bit off-putting to customers, suggested to Harry a blend of malt and acid. The restaurateur agreed and another step forward had been taken. "You can't really call it vinegar," cautioned Mr. Grimshaw. "Reight," laughed Harry, "we'll call it Ramsden bitter." His dripping came from Hemple Brothers, of Bingley, and his haddock and plaice from Drury's, of Grimsby, both chosen after painstaking research to find the very best.

While it is true, as his son has told us, that Harry was more interested in the state of the dustbins than the contents of the till, that does not mean that he was willing to be fleeced by his staff. On one occasion he noticed the top of a bin awaiting collection by the pig-swill man showed whole potatoes which seemed to Harry to be in prime condition, certainly not a suitable diet for pigs. He took two or three at random, put them through the chipper and discovered that each contained a two-bob piece slotted into the potato. One of his employees had devised a neat system of robbing the boss and spiriting the proceeds out in an ingenious, if noisome, style: half apiece for the thief and the swillman. The villain was detected and sacked; the swillman lost his contract. On another occasion, doing his rounds, Harry spotted the tail of a plaice protruding from the jacket pocket of one of the staff. He removed the fish and replaced it with fish-bits, bones, skin, and stuffed them not only into the pocket which had (partly) concealed the fish but into all the other pockets as well. That particular employee was not sacked. But he took the hint and thefts of fish came to an end.

Whit Walks

WHETHER by accident or design, Harry had chosen a perfect spot for his restaurant if one considers the matter of future development. It was at the junction of main roads out of Bradford and Leeds for anyone on the way to the Dales. He now produced methods of advertising his premises which were imaginative in the extreme. One of the most effective was also one of the cheapest. It centred on the then traditional Whitsuntide road-walking race which took contestants over a testing course starting in Manningham Lane, Bradford, and thence to Shipley, White Cross, Ilkley, Denton Park, Otley, Pool, Pool Bank, Rawdon, Apperley Bridge and back to Bradford, usually finishing in Peel Park. The crafty restaurateur used to buy a programme before the race started and check the number of walkers. If there were, say, 100 of them, he had a competitor's vest numbered 101 to be worn by Harry's own entrant, one Billy Robinson.

Billy was a man of many parts – a man who'd try owt, according to "young" Harry. Billy had worked on Blackpool's Golden Mile as a spieler, put in regular appearances as Father Christmas in Busby's grotto in Bradford (which makes me realise I must at some stage have been dangled on his knee while I told him what I hoped to get for *my* Christmas) and was generally game to turn his hand to anything. He was taken by car to Tranmere Park, Guiseley, and when the first genuine walkers were spotted climbing the long stretch of Hollins Hill, from Shipley to White Cross, Billy set off – fully accoutred as a contestant in the race – half a mile ahead of the field. There was always a big crowd watching in the area around the Ramsden emporium so that when the first walker came into view there was a hurried consulting of the programme: "Who is it in the lead? Number 101 – he's not listed here. Who can it be?" And then, as Billy streaked by at a cracking pace, knees and elbows flying, the spectators saw the legend he carried on his back: "A sure winner. Harry Ramsden's fish and chips."

His part in the race ended half a mile further on, at the Hare and Hounds, where Harry was waiting to pick up his walking advertisement, but just occasionally there were snags… like the time Harry's car broke down as he drove over Chevin End to the Hare and Hounds and Billy was left waiting on the wall ouside the pub while a friendly poultry-farmer, Joe Brown, helped to get the reluctant car started. Harry arrived full of embarrassed apologies but nothing worried Billy Robinson.

"No need to apologise, Harry," he smiled, unperturbed. "You wanted an advert; you've got it, buddy."

There was one occasion when young Lewis (Harry's nephew) was the look-out at Tranmere Park and failed to notice until the last minute that the leader of the race had reached the top of Hollins Hill. He was wearing a black vest and shorts instead of the expected white and a breathless Lewis rushed back to the car in which his cousin Harry ("young" Harry) was waiting with the unflappable Billy. "Get a move on or we'll all be i' bother," he gasped. "I never noticed yon feller until he were less than 'alf a mile away. If Billy isn't first past the shop, heads will roll." Young Harry switched on the engine as he turned to Billy: "You are now going to have your first flying start – about 30 miles an hour of a flying start." And he raced down to the main road and bundled out the fake competitor who made it to White Cross just ahead of the genuine article.

The years began to take their toll, however, and Billy one year found himself overtaken by the race leader as he struggled a little over that final half-mile to the Hare and Hounds. As his rival came abreast, not at all amused by the turn of events, he hissed at Billy, "What the bloody hell do you think you're doing?" Billy smiled gently at him as he replied, "It's all reight, lad. You just get on wi' your job and let me get on wi' mine."

Billy sounds to have been a lovely character; I do hope it *was* his knee I sat on during those never-to-be-forgotten Christmas visits to Santa's Grotto in Busby's Manningham Lane store.

Overleaf: **Here he comes – there he goes. Billy Robinson, who year-after-year was a bogus entrant in the Whitsuntide road race. It proved an extremely effective form of advertising.**

A Born Showman

IF there were not too many privately-owned motor cars on the road (as children in the 1920s and even into the 1930s we used to note the "makes" of cars and their registration numbers in little books), there were buses and there were bicycles to take people out of their cramped and claustrophobic week-day lives. Even while he was setting up the original wooden hut premises which was the immediate predecessor of the modern Harry Ramsden's, the future fish-and-chip tycoon was standing at the top of Hollins Hill watching perspiring cyclists and hikers reach the brow and musing, "They'll be fair gagged. I'll bet they'd give owt for a bottle of pop while they have a rest." So his niece Edith was installed in a little caravan at the top of the hill, selling bottles of mineral water, packets of crisps, bars of chocolate. He never missed a trick.

When his grand design finally took shape at White Cross, Harry reasoned that the people venturing out into the country would inevitably have a brood of children with them. On the field behind his restaurant (now a car park) he set up swings and roundabouts and miniature golf. But other people did *that*. Indeed, in my own boyhood in Keighley I remember the delight with which we undertook family outings to beauty spots on the hills and in the wooded river-valleys around the town – Newsholme Dene, Benson's, Goyt Stock – where the parents could buy jugs of tea to drink with the picnic sandwiches and the kids could disport themselves on swings and roundabouts or paddle in a stream. They are the happiest of my childhood memories before television was even heard of and not all families had a wireless. Harry Ramsden went one better. At week-ends he arranged band concerts where his older customers could sit on the grass behind the restaurant and listen. For the children he decked out a little bull-nosed Morris car in the trappings of a boat, called it the Saucy Sally, and for a penny the youngsters – whose parents could never dream of being well-enough off ever to contemplate a ride in a car – were driven around the field. Even that wasn't enough for the master showman. He dressed up the captain of his ship in naval uniform and all went well until skipper Billy Robinson spliced the mainbrace a little too

Entertainments at White Cross, all part of Harry Ramsden's grand design to bring in the crowds.

Above: At weekends, customers could sit on the grass behind the restaurant and listen to brass band concerts.

Left: Billy Robinson was dressed up in naval uniform in order to captain Saucy Sally, a bull-nosed Morris car decked out in the trappings of a boat.

Below: Saucy Sally is on the left of this picture; on the right a queue is forming to partake in another entertainment – clock golf.

enthusiastically one day and took a delighted crew of young passengers careering down the main road on a completely unauthorised and unscheduled "cruise".

But even the week-end revellers, young and old, were only a small part of the Ramsden clientele at White Cross. From the first, Harry set his sights firmly on the mill trade of Guiseley, and while the restaurant was the place which attracted visitors from afar it was the outsales to local industry which gave Harry Ramsden's its sound financial footing. Bulk orders came in daily from Peats Mill, Moons Mill, Crompton Parkinson (electrical goods and fittings) and Silver Cross (perambulators) – firms with hundreds of employees who were only too happy to have a variation on their sandwich-diet at lunchtime. This, of course, happened all over the West Riding in the twenties and thirties; many fish-and-chip shops enjoyed the patronage of mill-workers in different trades, especially on Fridays, which was and still is, a traditional fish-and-chip-lunch-day in industrial Yorkshire. But few mills had the luxury of a local shop which was open for lunch every day of the week and now offered *a delivery service*. The custom was for a junior worker to be despatched to the local fisheries to place an order, earlier in the day, for a bulk supply at a specified time. (It was hard luck if you happened to be a "domestic" customer waiting for a humble fish and a penn'orth when an overall-clad emissary arrived for his ordered "25 times".) Harry Ramsden imposed no such extra burdens. So long as the order was placed in advance, the food was now delivered by one Harry Sugden, riding a Triumph motor-bike and sidecar piled high with packages. The restaurant was a secondary consideration in Ramsden's early trading days. That was for the posh end of the clientele for it cost a shilling to sit down and be served with fish-and-chips, tea and bread and butter. From the outsales the charge was a penny for fish and a ha'penny for chips – delivered to the mill! That price was restored when the whole emporium celebrated its 21st birthday on 7th July, 1952, even though the normal charge had by that time increased a bit since the establishment opened. On that July evening the queue was four deep half a mile down the road to the Hare and Hounds public house and five miles the other way, at the Horsforth roundabout, police were turning back buses and cars with the advice, "You'll never get through for t'crowds at Harry Ramsden's".

For someone who proved himself a born showman, Harry Ramsden was self-effacing in the extreme in his personal life; for a man who could not bear to be cheated out of a penny, he proved a generous friend to many. In short, like most of us, he was a mass of contradictions. Once he had become prosperous, he had

34

Harry Ramsden – a born showman.

his shoes hand-made as well as his suits and shirts, yet he was anything but a Beau Brummell. It was as if everything he wore had been tailored specifically to help him merge into the background. The suits were made from identical bolts of cloth so it would appear to the casual observer that Harry wore the same suit for years and years! His family cannot remember a time when he ever went into a shop for *anything*. He never ate in his own restaurant, preferring to sit in a small room at the back used for storing cleaning materials. Harry junior never knew his father to ride on a bus. There was always a family car but it was as unpretentious as almost everything else in his life, usually an Austin Seven, a Morris Minor or a Wolseley Wasp. Just once he bought a gleaming Lea Francis – but he never drove it.

The last thing he wanted, it seemed, was to be recognised as *the* Harry Ramsden, owner and mastermind behind the world's most famous fish restaurant. Not for him any strutting about with a grand proprietorial air. Harry was more likely to be found with a broom, sweeping up stray papers outside the shop. Sometimes (before his carpark had been tarmacadamed with white space-lines painted) he acted as a parking attendant to persuade his more affluent customers – as anyone with a car had to be – to park in orderly lines and it was on one such occasion that a motorist handed him a sixpenny tip, a princely sum in the thirties, with the consoling words, "'Ere th'art, lad. I don't suppose yon bugger i' theer pays thi much". The magnate pocketed the money without comment, reflecting that he never looked a gift horse in the mouth.

If he had a trade mark (other than the vast emporium at White Cross) it would have had to be his flat 'at – his cap. Harry was rarely seen without it, or his stiff winged collar. When his daughter Shirley was married in church at Burley-in-Wharfedale with a really pukka reception at the Craiglands Hotel in Ilkley, she wanted her family to be formally dressed in morning coats and grey toppers. Her father shuddered, and flatly refused. "You can have your wedding with all the trimmings, lass, and I'll pay for it all, but I am not getting dressed up."

Did the man *ever* relax? Did he find the need to get away from the pressures of business – and, as we have seen, he created new pressures for himself every day – and forget for a few hours the world of catering? The answer is: "Very rarely". Even on an outing to Blackpool, which he enjoyed, he could not resist taking "young" Harry into a fish-and-chip shop and pointing out triumphantly how the fish "plopped" dully into the fat instead of meeting the fierce, sizzling reception which would have indicated that the oil (not dripping in Lancashire) was at a lower temperature than that Harry insisted upon.

At Blackpool in a landau, with Harry Ramsden seated at the back. The small boy is nephew Harry Corbett, later in life to achieve national fame through Sooty.

Once a year, at August Bank Holiday, he put young Harry in the car, picked up his sister Florrie and her husband Jim Corbett, together with young Harry Corbett, and his brother Leslie (who used to play the saxophone and clarinet at local dances and clubs), and took them to Blackpool, to Mrs. Carr's in Cavendish Road. There he left his relatives and drove back to attend to business, returning a week later to pick them up after their holiday. But it was one aspect of the outward trip which has fascinated "young" Harry for more than 50 years and it is one which gives us an indication of how his father, just occasionally, liked a bit of style. Let the small boy's memory tell us the story:

"Before we set off my Dad used to ring up the Commercial Hotel at Gisburn. It was a three-hour trip to Blackpool in those days so this was a sort of half-way stopping-off spot and our breakfast was ordered for ten o'clock exactly. But it wasn't served in the dining room. We had a private room, and the breakfast would be brought in on silver-plated trays – slices of best ham, eggs, tomatoes, mushrooms... oooh, it was marvelous."

The elder Harry was probably never happier than when he went to a favourite spot beside the River Wharfe, near Pool. He bought a small caravan, equipped it in spartan fashion with the bare essentials – a deck chair, a Calor gas-ring, a kettle and a tea-pot. From the shop he took with him a cold piece of fried fish and a buttered teacake. And on a day there in the sunshine, listening to the murmur of the stream with his newspaper to read (or to drape over his head if the sun was too hot), he found peace – wonderful in its simplicity.

He had brought in a manager – Eddie Stokes, an experienced caterer from Blackpool, in 1954 – and he had chosen his staff with care over many years. Now at last, with the business firmly re-established after the war and Harry drifting into his sixties, he felt he was ready to take a rest from time to time. It had been a long, hard haul.

Twenty-First Birthday

A never-to-be-forgotten day was July 7th, 1952, when the White Cross emporium celebrated its twenty-first birthday. It became known as "penny-ha'penny day", fish being sold at a penny and chips at a halfpenny – the prices charged by Grandfather Harry when he founded the Ramsden fish-and-chip empire prior to the first world war.

Yorkshire folk, never slow to scent a bargain, flocked to Guiseley and queues formed for miles. Fortunately, the occasion was recorded in a splendid series of photographs, a selection of which is reproduced on this and the following pages.

Harry Ramsden puts the clock back forty years and for one day sells fish-and-chips at the prices charged in 1912.

39

Above: The "Big Fry" begins.

Left: Just some of the crowds thronging round White Cross.

Above: **Harry Ramsden with twins Mavis and Wendy Raistrick of Horsforth, first in the "outsales" queue.**

Right: **Harry obliges a group of autograph seekers.**

Above: Harry Corbett helps to entertain the crowds.

Opposite, top: A magnificent firework display provided a grand finale.

Opposite, bottom: The band played on, well into the night.

Young Lewis and Young Harry

LEWIS, son of Grandfather Harry's eldest son (also Lewis), shared with his many cousins, uncles and aunts a strong sense of family and in many ways he is the official chronicler of their history. He had a remarkable memory for trivia, loved to tell a tale and there can be little doubt that amongst his contemporaries (and certainly those less gifted as raconteurs) he would be known as "a reight windbag". He could take a single incident in his life, or that of his Uncle Harry or Great Uncle Charlie, and weave it into a narrative so rich in illustrative detail that the telling could be dragged out into half an hour or more without apparent effort.

Lewis, a call boy at the Bradford Alhambra Theatre in his early teens, was a most reluctant recruit to the fish-and-chip trade, partly because he nurtured a life-long belief that he was capable of better things and overwhelmingly because at an impressionable age he had had a taste of life in The Theatre and he never ceased to regret a lost opportunity to follow that path. Fifty years afterwards he recalled, with a sadness in every cadence, the time when he lost the chance to tread the boards of the variety theatres of Britain as part of Will Hay's schoolroom. Hay (1888-1949) was a character comedian who specialised in the role of a schoolmaster of endearingly bumbling incompetence. After many years on the halls he turned to films, starring in nearly twenty of them between 1934 and 1944, not always as a schoolmaster but playing characters which were always a variation on that basic theme of farcical inadequacy. Who can say what course young Lewis Ramsden's life might have taken if he had been allowed to take up an offer from Hay's manager to become one of the teacher's lively (and equally incompetent) pupils? No less an authority than Leslie Halliwell described Hay as "one of the screen's greats" and awarded him the rosette which admitted the actor to Halliwell's Hall of Fame with the citation: "For developing an unforgettable comic persona which lives in the memory independently of his films; and for persuading us to root for that character despite its basically unsympathetic nature". Such was the man young Lewis was invited to join on the stage; it remained the major tragedy of his life that his father would not let him go.

With a pathos which is almost heart-breaking he recalled, half a century later, "Fish-and-chips prevailed once more". It was said with more sadness than bitterness, even though his father administered the final blow by removing Lewis from the Alhambra Theatre and installing him in the humblest junior role in the fish-and-chip trade, that of the chip-chopper. If Lewis had been a frustrated actor, deprived of the one means he sought of expressing himself, it might have been easier for him to bear. He could at least then have railed at a dated but inflexible concept of family loyalty and commitment. But he did not see himself as an actor so much as a man of the theatre, a man excited more by the smell of the greasepaint than the roar of the crowd. He loved contact with the great contemporary personalities of the Music Hall and he never forgot one detail, however minute or seemingly insignificant, of his days amongst them.

"I would have worked there for nothing," he reminisced. "When I called 'Overture and beginners' I was calling it to Marie Lloyd, Nellie Wallace, to George Robey and Rob Wilton and to George Formby – not the man who made a fortune in Blackpool and on the screen with his ukelele and his gormlessness, but *his* father, a lovely man. He suffered from asthma, I remember, which made him braver than ever in my eyes to go on stage night after night. One night he asked me to go to the papershop across the road because the young lady there had promised to make him a bit of supper. I brought it back on a tray, all neatly laid out and started to leave the dressing-room but he called me back. 'I can't eat all this by myself,' he said. 'You'll have to help me out.' So there was I, a lad of fifteen, eating supper in his dressing-room with one of the great music hall personalities of his day. But so many of them were kind people with great, generous hearts and long memories.

"Take Nellie Wallace, for instance. In the days before she topped the bill she had stayed with Uncle Harry and Auntie Beaty when my aunt let rooms to theatricals. Nellie had been ill during her week at the Alhambra and Auntie Beaty made her some beef tea which she swore had been responsible for her recovery. Years later she came back to the Alhambra and, learning that I was the nephew, she told me, 'Tell your aunt and uncle to come and see the show as my guests and to have dinner with me afterwards. Oh yes, and ask your aunt if she will bring me some of her beef tea.' She did."

The memories came flooding back to young Lewis. He was fascinated by an act which involved "a man with a sealion", and with the orchestra playing softly

"It's three o'clock in the morning", the man would be returning home from a night on the town with a set of plasterboard painted buildings, a lamp-post and a dustbin. The drunk rummaged in the dustbin, pulled out an old top hat and the sealion, emerging from the other side of the stage, pounced on the hat and went into a full routine of balancing the hat on the tip of his nose, flipping it and catching it and voicing its own approval of the trick (and its reward of a fish) by clapping its fins and honking with delight. Playing the Alhambra on the same bill were a highly temperamental lady singer called Daisy Dormer and the comedian Rob Wilton. There was no love lost between those two as indeed there was none between Ms Dormer and the orchestra, the programme boys, usherettes and chocolate-sellers. Daisy was entirely likely to stop the orchestra in mid-bar and tell them that she could manage better without them. She would stop in mid-song and order the programme boys not to ply their trade while she was singing. She was not a lovable lady at all.

One evening, while she was in full cry on stage, young Lewis, pursuing his fascination with the sea-lion while it was sleeping peacefully in its box, was startled by the tip-toe approach of Rob Wilton with finger to his lips, urging silence. Slowly, he pulled a fish out of his pocket and waved it over the box. In seconds the sea-lion had awakened, clamouring for its prize; on stage, not ten yards away, Ms Dormer – at climax point in a tender and sentimental ballad – was interrupted by raucous honking and frantic flapping of Pinnipeddian flippers. She flounced off the stage, denouncing the "filthy stinking beast" and all those who found it necessary to appear in the theatre with such creatures, and vowing never to appear again on the same bill as the now-hysterical Mr. Wilton.

It was from Bob Anderson and his polo pony that young Lewis learned a secret which baffled theatre audiences for years – how a horse could provide the answers to simple arithmetical problems called out from the auditorium.

"Bob Anderson held the horse by the head and stood a little in front of it with one leg slightly bent," he explained. "If the sum was, say, take eight from fourteen, he would then flex his leg straight six times and the pony, observing this, then tapped its hoof six times." But what intrigued the teenager even more was a ritual performed by the immaculate Mr. Anderson each evening – "his boots shone so you could actually see your face in them" – when he asked to be called precisely fifteen minutes before he was due on stage. He would then take the pony outside the stage door, strip himself down to the waist in best "All Creatures Great and Small" fashion and (it's difficult to put it any more delicately than this) give it an

Lewis senior (right), probably photographed at Blackpool. Behind the bar are Harry Ramsden and his wife Beatrice.

enema. Everything about Bob Anderson was pristine and hygienic. Or perhaps he didn't want to soil his highly-polished boots?

Nothing from those backstage days was too insignificant to be dismissed from young Lewis's memory. It is perhaps not difficult to understand why he recalled so vividly the sight of Margo Joyce ("a real spanking lady") in her briefs but no bra when he returned from an errand to get her "a bottle of port wine", but, fifty years on, he remembered the exact extent of tips he received at the end of the week – ten shillings from Neil Kenyon, a Scot extraordinary, and another ten bob from Marie Lloyd, who was known to hand out three or four pounds to be shared amongst the scene-shifters. Lewis's love affair with the music hall was a passionate one. When his father decreed that not only could he not travel the country as one of Will Hay's pupils but he must give up his job as call boy as well it broke his heart. But he did not, in any of his reminiscences, ever mention a fleeting thought of disobeying, of going his own way. Children didn't do that when Lewis was a lad – not from a sense of fear but simply from a sense of duty to the family.

Lewis's apprenticeship in the fish-and-chip trade had, in fact, started (even though he didn't know it at the time) when he was a mere toddler. His father, Lewis senior, had been pressed into service in the family shop by Grandfather Harry, that stern patriarch, as had all other members of the family as we have seen, except the Harry who is the central figure in this family history. Lewis junior watched his father lead a slave-like existence in the shop at 22 Manchester Road which was open on most days of the year. Lewis senior had to be at the fish market at 5 a.m. to buy supplies; he returned to Manchester Road to clean and prepare the fish, light the coal-burning, one-pan frying range, then supervise the frying. After the lunchtime trade the shop and range had to be cleaned and the fish prepared for the evening session. Then, after more cleaning, he would return home about midnight, ready to start the daily round and common task all over again at 5 a.m. His day off was Tuesday – after buying, cleaning and preparing the fish and pre-frying it to be ready for the lunchtime trade the remainder of the day was then his own!

Yet all was not dross and serfdom. On Saturdays, Lewis senior was allowed a fortnightly visit to watch Bradford City play and Lewis junior, from the earliest days he could remember, went with him. Sadly, he rememers that they never saw a game finish in all those years they went to Valley Parade. "We had to leave at threequarter-time to be ready in the shop for the tea-time trade with shoppers – and those who had been lucky enough to see the football match to its finish," he mourned. And here again we are grateful to the photographic memory of young Lewis. "Once, I remember City had been playing the team later to become Leicester City but at that time known as Leicester Fosse. It was a particularly exciting game and my Dad couldn't resist staying a few minutes longer than we should have done. When we rushed breathlessly back to the shop, Grandfather Harry had not found it necessary to start preparations himself. *That* had to wait until my Dad returned. So when the first customers started filing in and found no fish-and-chips ready they were entertained during their wait by Granddad's heavy sarcasm: "What, fish-and-chips? There's nowt ready yet, I can tell thi'. Didn't tha knaw Bradford City were at home? Tha mustn't expect to get thi tea on time when City are at home, tha knaws. Today they were playing Leicester Fosse (but

Grandfather Harry, an unlettered man and not a football fan, could not get his tongue round the name and it came out something like Lafotesser) so tha' can't expect thi fish and chips at t'usual time, can tha?"

Lewis senior's wage for this week-long drudgery was 28s a week (£1.40 in modern money) and he had given up "a good job" on the tramways to obey the patriarchal summons to 22 Manchester Road. It seems rather more than hard that when Grandfather Harry died and Lewis attempted, with sister Florrie, to run his own fish-and-chip business in Manchester Road he was beset by the most cruel misfortunes. First, the lease of the shop was bought over his head and when he moved into other premises further up Manchester Road he had a heart attack and died beside his own frying range. It was a sad end to what must have been a pretty miserable life.

"Young" Harry had, in many ways, a strange and lonely boyhood. His mother was an invalid from the time he was born and he has scarcely any memory of her. His step-mother, it seemed, did not like him and in his formative years his father was busily concerned in building up the White Cross restaurant. It was a relief and a delight to young Harry when he was sent off to Blackpool to live with his aunt – his father's sister, Annie. The boy had spent his earliest years at White Cross sleeping in a caravan with the windows wide open, winter and summer, to try to ward off the TB which had killed his mother and there were times when he was not expected to survive. Indeed, when he went to tell his father during the Second World War that he intended to join up, Harry looked incredulously at his son and commented, "Join up? They'll never take thee for t' *Salvation* Army."

Annie, too, had chest problems and it was her brother who bought ("for £350, brand new") a house at 35 Brentwood Avenue, Anchorsholme, Cleveleys, where she went to live to get the benefit of the clean seaside air. This is where young Harry spent his teenage years, cycling to and from a local grammar school and gradually shaking off the frailty of his earlier childhood. After leaving school he joined the Merchant Navy, working for the United Towing Company of Hull, and it was during this time – the early days of World War II – that he was offered a job in trawlers which took him from the east coast back to the west, to Fleetwood, and so, to his great joy, he was able to live once more at the home of Auntie Annie. The job had its appeal, too, when he was given £3 a day subsistence allowance while waiting for a berth on a trawler to become available: "Three pound a day for doin' nowt." It was a different story, however, when he finally went to sea and savoured the delights of a deckhand's work, trying to snatch a few hours sleep

"Young" Harry (left), with his father, the second Mrs Ramsden and their daughter Shirley.

between the four-hour trawls, then embarking on the frenzied task of cutting up and cleaning the catch as the nets went over the side once again.

It was almost a relief to join the Royal Navy and get a posting to the shore-based *HMS Victory* at Portsmouth as an officers' chef but then came a sea-going spell of duty in the destroyer *HMS Keppel* which had a notable wartime history. After that he joined a new destroyer *HMS Gore* with the hazardous job of anti-submarine patrol in the Atlantic, ahead of convoys. It was by no means a comfortable war for the young man.

What of cousin Lewis in the meantime? His stage ambitions frustrated, Lewis turned his attention to football and spent some time playing with Bradford Park

Avenue second eleven which was not a full-time professional engagement. After the death of his father he made a trip to London, with Uncle Harry's support, to explore the possibility of opening a fish-and-chip shop in the capital – of preaching the Gospel according to Harry Ramsden in parts where they had not heard The Word. He came back fired with enthusiasm – at least for life in what was then the world's biggest and greatest city.

"Eee, you've niver seen owt like it," he told his uncle. "There's trains that run under t'ground and there's a place called Lyons Corner House. It's marvellous. A restaurant on five floors and an orchestra playin' on all of 'em. There's nowt like it i' Bradford, I can tell thi."

He had heard, between sight-seeing in the West End, of a shop which might be for sale on Highbury Hill and Lewis' eyes lit up. "Highbury?" Highbury meant the mighty Arsenal Football Club and a football club meant crowds – crowds who knew nothing of the wonders of West Yorkshire fish-and-chips. Lewis went into business, advertising his shop as selling fish "guaranteed without a bone". That had to be a winner in London where they knew nothing of haddock fillets fried in beef dripping. After a slow start, Lewis gradually built up a promising trade and then the war intervened in his life, too. He drove huge transporters for the Gloster Aircraft Company and it gave him at least two "tales" which he recorded for posterity before he died.

He was called up to take the RAF's first jet plane, the Gloster Meteor, from Gloucester to Scotland and the company went to the most elaborate lengths to check on the height and width of roads and bridges between the West of England and the Scottish border to ensure there were no hitches. Everything was checked and double-checked down to the last detail but they forgot just one point of the route – the gate out of the factory where the aircraft had been assembled. It wouldn't go through, and the whole entrance had to be demolished!

During the long, slow progress northwards, Lewis took advantage of an overnight halt to visit Uncle Harry at White Cross.

"What's tha doin', then?" inquired Harry, companionably.

"I'm takkin' an aeroplane to Scotland on a truck and tha' should see it. It flies wi'out any propellers."

"No propellers? Don't be so bloody daft," responded his uncle, and returned to the eminently more sensible business of selling fish-and-chips.

Lewis' London shop had gone when he returned after the war and though he had made a reasonable success of it his heart was never in it. "Wi' fish-and-chips,"

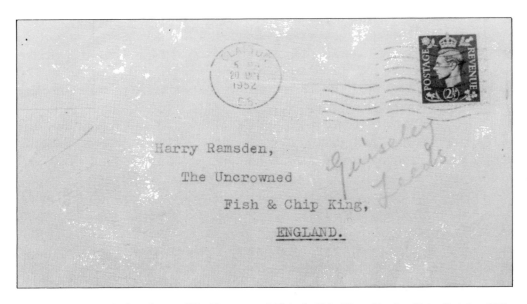

Harry Ramsden,

The Uncrowned

Fish & Chip King,

ENGLAND.

The letter, posted in London to "The Uncrowned Fish & Chip King, England" on October 20th, 1952, and delivered to Guiseley two days later.

he said, "You're either making a mess or clearing one up." And that, in realistic, unromanticised terms, just about sums it up. Fortunately for the world his uncle took a longer view.

Harry senior could never quite credit the extent of his fame and it was young Lewis who insisted to him, during one of his uncle's visits to London, that a letter addressed to "Harry Ramsden, the uncrowned fish-and-chip king, England", would be delivered without problems. They wrote out the envelope, posted it and it was delivered to White Cross two days later.

Dancing in the Dark

LIKE most successful business men, Harry knew that he could not afford to stand still yet while he certainly had the Midas touch as far as fish-and-chips (and one or two other enterprises) were concerned, not everything he touched turned immediately to gold. But all along the line one has to admire his adventurous spirit. The 200-seater restaurant must have seemed an enormous gamble in itself to so many hard-headed West Riding folk, yet no sooner had it got into its stride than Harry was trying his hand at being an entertainments impresario. He rented a large building just beyond the White Cross public house, along Bradford Road, to stage dances, boxing and wrestling bills, contests to find the best pair of waltzers in the district, then exponents of the foxtrot, the quickstep. None of it worked – but it wasn't for the want of trying as Harry might have said himself.

It all started out as "Ramsden's Dance Assembly", and then became successively the White Cross Ballroom, the Spanish Vineyard, the Blue Kitten Club – names designed to capture the imagination of the public and to lure them into Harry Ramsden's latest venture, but somehow none of it ever took off. It is difficult to understand why, because in this pre-television era ballroom dancing was highly popular as participant entertainment and, of course, Harry hoped that the crowds which he anticipated would flock to his dance assembly would take in supper at his restaurant, so he was taking a double chance. It really got under way on August Bank Holiday, 1932, and for an outlay of 15 shillings (75p) for a special announcement in the *Yorkshire Observer,* Bradford's daily morning paper in those days, he got himself a little editorial "plug" as well: "A splendid holiday programme has been arranged at Ramsden's Dance Assembly, White Cross, Guiseley, where a carnival dance will be held from 8.30 pm on Monday to 1 am Tuesday. This should be a thoroughly enjoyable event for many attractions have been arranged, including a 'stop trot' competition and other novelties. Music will be provided by Stanley Broughton's Mayfair Orchestra. Admission is 1/6d (7½p) and there is a free car park. Special late buses will be run for the function."

As summer gave way to autumn of that year we find Mr. Karl Mayer, and his partner, Miss J. Sacks, both of Leeds, winning the quickstep competition "in a close finish" (*Wharfedale Observer*) and the foxtrot prize being carried off by Mr. Raymond Graham and Miss D. Bracken, of Bradford. In September, Mr. Richard Moss, of Bradford, partnered by Miss Sally Shawsmith, of Kirkstall, won the novices waltz competition and the *Wharfedale Observer* reported that judging the dancing by popular vote of the audience was highly successful.

But somehow it did not attract the crowds Harry had hoped to see; not even the engagement of Charles and Veronica, Yorkshire's Premier Danseurs, provided a full house. By mid-January the Dance Assembly had become "the White Cross Roadhouse" and was advertising the "special engagement of Billy Reid and his famous Havana Band, from the New Victoria, Bradford", to provide the music for a non-stop carnival night. Harry spared no expense with his advertising both for the dancing and the boxing/wrestling nights. Apart from the normal announcement type of ads he ventured into the Personal Column of the *Telegraph and Argus*: "Jesse, sorry could not come to the White Cross Roadhouse last Saturday. Tomorrow certain; Hilda and all the girls are coming. Charlie." Harry had now developed a taste for colourful advertising and we find the West Yorkshire Bus Company joining in: "No Need to Ride Past. All West Yorkshire buses stop at the White Cross Roadhouse. Dancing de luxe every Saturday." And next, he waxed lyrical:

> "What we Says is:
> Life Ain't All You Want
> But It's All You 'Ave,
> So 'Ave it.
> Stick a Geranium In Yer 'At
> Come to Guiseley
> And Be 'Appy."

Announcements flooded into the offices of the Bradford and District Newspaper Company Ltd; Harry Ramsden must have been their favourite client:

> TWO YEARS HARD LABOUR
> but the result has been worth it.
> THE WHITE CROSS ROADHOUSE
> is now leading with Saturday dancing.
> See for yourself any week-end.

And then: "We don't say we have the best dance hall in this city, we are too modest. But as we are truthful we must tell you there isn't a better."

The Spanish Vineyard, alias the White Cross Ballroom. It was one of the very few Harry Ramsden ventures that never really succeeded.

Harry had found a new metier. He could have walked into any 1932/33 advertising agency as a copywriter. But he couldn't make the clients walk into his dance assembly, Roadhouse, Vineyard, Blue Kitten, whatever he called it. He extended his advertising to the *Yorkshire Evening Post,* lavishing 16 shillings (80p) on a 16-line announcement and sadly totted up in his account book for the first week in January 1934 a total of £2 2s 6d outlay to newspapers, £3 3s for the band, 3s 9d for heating, 10s for lighting and 4s for cleaning. With other small items the total expenditure came to £7 13s 3d. Alongside those figures, Harry has mournfully recorded takings of £6 3s 9d, giving him a net loss of £1 9s 6d.

But he wasn't beaten yet. Back came the Premier Danseurs, Charles and Veronica, together with Harry Paver and His Band of Six Star Musicians. Advertising revenue was lavished upon the *Telegraph and Argus,* the *Yorkshire Evening Post,* weekly newspapers in Ilkley, Otley and Burley plus a slide shown on the screen of the Guiseley Picture House. The result was takings of £6 8s 8d, expenses of £8 5s 3d – a loss of £1 16s 7d. He tried reduced admission prices before 8 pm: ladies 6d, gents 9d (it was 1s and 1s 6d after eight) and then took the unprecedented step of offering FREE admission to one person on presentation of a notice cut out of a newspaper. But Harry wasn't daft; that announcement only appeared in a small-circulation weekly paper! Nevertheless, the end product was another loss, this time of £2 10s 3d.

It obviously could not continue but Harry Ramsden was not a man to give up easily. He turned to Sunday dancing but, knowing the pitfalls of a Lord's Day

Observance Act, strictly enforced in the 1930s, he took all available legal advice. He had reasoned that one cause of the failure of his Wednesday and Saturday night dances was the existence of so much competition in the area. Now, if he could get round the law and provide dancing on *Sunday* he might well be on a winner. So his next move was to form a members-only club (subscriptions 2s) for the purpose of enjoying ballroom dancing. This resulted in a trenchant article of rebuke in his parish magazine by the Rector of Guiseley, Archdeacon Howson, and shortly after it appeared the County Prosecuting Solicitor's Department at Wakefield issued 27 summonses against Harry, as club secretary, and eight of his associates in the management of the club. It was a cause celebre when they all appeared at Otley Magistrates' Court but there was no way that Harry was going down without a fight.

He engaged to represent the nine of them a legendary figure in Northern jurisprudence, the redoubtable Alf Masser, who was the Perry Mason of his day in West Riding Courts. And characteristically, Mr. Masser started the day with a dramatic submission to the magistrates: he objected to the presence on the Bench of... Canon Howson! In its own time, this was a sensational courtroom ploy but, of course, it should have been perfectly obvious to the justices that a man who had publicly stated his opposition to the Sunday dancing could not be allowed to sit in judgement on the defendants. The Archdeacon himself should certainly have known this but he innocently asked Mr. Masser: "Have I done or said anything that will prejudice the case?"

With proper respect (but, I suspect, a huge and delighted inward chuckle), Alf replied, "I have read something in a magazine under your pen relative to certain things on Sundays and which you have written."

The Rector conceded the point and then left the Bench to sit in the body of the court. The hearing continued, and ended with a dismissal of all the summonses. One suspects that it gave Harry Ramsden enough satisfaction to compensate for his losses on the dance assembly. He was a peaceable and law-abiding citizen who liked to be left to get on with running his businesses. But if Authority frowned upon his activities he was not unhappy to take up the challenge.

At one time he gave one of the fields adjoining the restaurant – not at that time converted into a car park – to "young" Harry who promptly agreed to a request from an Otley businessman to hold an exhibition of tents in the field. This brought a prompt and pompous letter from the Clerk to Aireborough Council demanding to know from Harry senior why he was staging the display without permission of the local authority. Harry waited a couple of days before replying mildly that he had no display of tents taking place on any field of his. Back came a peremptory inquiry: "Whose field is it, then, if it is not yours? As far as we are concerned, you are the owner." After another day or two Harry replied that the field was owned by his son and this brought another thunderous communication from the Clerk (no doubt fuming by this time): "Well, tell your son to remove the tents."

It was one of the joyous moments of Harry's life when he was able (after the usual, suitable interval) to inquire, "What tents?" The exhibition had now ended; there was not a marquee in sight in the vicinity of Harry Ramsden's restaurant. Can there be a Yorkshireman alive who does not recognise, and delight in, this small victory over Authority?

The Proudest of Yorkshiremen

HARRY Ramsden was not, in the general sense, a gregarious man, and as we have seen he disliked ostentation and self-promotion. At the same time he gave – and received in return – great loyalty from employees, associates and a select circle of close, personal friends. And he liked to enjoy the good things in life when he felt he had earned them; he liked to do things with a certain degree of style whether they were on a grand scale or a minor one. Thus – Friday was the night when he picked up young Harry after school and took him, along with his step-mother, for high tea at Collinson's Cafe or the County Hotel in Bradford and a visit to the New Victoria Cinema with double-feature shows and an organ recital as well. Above all he loved Laurel and Hardy films but when he turned his attention to drama he like his "heavies" to be *really* heavy, with Edward G. Robinson as the favourite, followed by James Cagney and George Raft. He admired the English actors George Arliss and Charles Laughton. He had no time for frivolities such as romance.

When television became part of our national entertainment diet after the war Harry yearned to be the first man in the district to own a set – but how to get a picture? At first, reception was only possible in the London area but as it gradually crept northwards, with the erection of the transmitting mast at Sutton Coldfield, Harry seized his chance. He bought a small plot of land above Hawksworth, high on the edge of Ilkley Moor (which he loved passionately) and installed a caravan there. Then he had his own power supply connected, which meant running a cable about a quarter of a mile from the nearest point, and despatched young Harry to Guiseley Post Office where they had never even seen a TV licence! But they got one, and another as well. No. 1 licence-holder in Guiseley was Harry Ramsden, and No. 2 was Willie Wilson from the Silver Cross perambulator works who had also hit on the idea of siting an aerial on a south-facing plot of high ground. Harry was tickled pink by his new toy and spent hours in the caravan watching the programmes put out by the BBC television service. He confided in his son,

"What a life you are going to have with t'developments you are going to see in t'next 50 years". How right he was, even if he didn't live to see many of them, but... "aeroplanes without propellers" were only just the beginning.

He never saw colour TV and he never knew the magic of the remote-control apparatus, Teletext or the immense scope of outside broadcasts. But he was happy with what he had.

Such was the fame of his restaurant that there is no doubt he could have made a big thing out of visits by internationally-known personalities but Harry did not court celebrity status. What he did value was the friendship of people who might well be famous in their own right but simply accepted him and liked him for himself. Barney Colehan,the BBC producer, who gave us first of all "Have a Go" on radio, was one of these. When Barney turned to television production he successively dreamed up vehicles for "cousin" Sooty, then "It's a Knock-out" and its continental development, "Jeux Sans Frontieres" and the phenomenally-succesful "The Good Old Days", which, when it was finally laid to rest after 30 years, had a waiting list of 25,000 people who had hoped to be included, one day, in the audience. Barney lived close to the Ramsden restaurant and each Sunday morning he went to Larwood House for pre-lunch gin and tonics and a weekly chat.

Through Barney, Harry was introduced to the legendary Wilfred Pickles and almost at once another great friendship developed; their letters to each other are a treasured part of the family album. Willie Smith, the billiards and snooker star, was another pal for many years and Harry paid many visits to the Thurston Hall in London to watch him play exhibition matches with Joe and Fred Davis and Walter Lindrum while not neglecting to import Willie to the Guiseley Bowling Club to put on exhibitions there. Like virtually every other Yorkshireman, he loved his cricket and two of the most regular pre-war customers were Hedley Verity and Bill Bowes, that great bowling duo (with their own close friendship), while in the post-war era a young man grew up in the family home barely 100 yards away from the White Cross restaurant who was destined to captain Yorkshire and England – Brian Close. Many have been the evenings after a day's play at Park Avenue or Headingley that Brian, Len Shackleton (that marvellous footballer with Bradford, Newcastle United and Sunderland, afterwards a *Daily Express* sports-writer) and myself have rushed up to Bradford Golf Club at Hawksworth for nine holes followed by supper from "Harry's".

Harry, as we have remarked, enjoyed a bit of style in his outings and for visits

61

to snooker exhibitions at Thurston Hall he followed a ritual: the Yorkshire Pullman from Leeds station, breakfast on the train followed by a couple of drinks, overnight at the Regent Palace Hotel. On one occasion as the visiting party prepared to go out for a meal (Harry, his second wife, and "young" Harry), the junior Ramsden flagged down a taxi which was in the process of dropping a passenger at the Regent Palace. Young Harry caught a glimpse of the man inside the cab and gasped, "Don't get out. Just wait there a minute if you will," and raced off in search of father, dragging him outside. "Well, I'll be blowed," said the two men, simultaneously. The passenger was Willie Smith, the man they had come to see play snooker. So they all had dinner together before the evening session.

Internationally-known personalities regularly visited the restaurant, even though Harry Ramsden did not court celebrity status.

Left: **Sooty and cousin Harry Corbett.**

Above: **Wilfred Pickles and Mabel "have a go" at Harry Ramsden's.**

So much for the glamour of the bright lights. Harry Ramsden had an equal – probably greater – affection for the simpler pleasures of life. He liked nothing better than to take out the family pet dog, Teddy, up Thorpe Lane, through Hawksworth village and right over the edge of Ilkley Moor to Dick Hudson's, the pub above Eldwick. Then after a convivial rest and fortified by a hot rum toddy, the pair would walk back, in rain, hail, snow or sunshine. And to young Harry his father would say, "You can't beat that. This is the most beautiful place in the world and we are lucky to live here." In the most simplistic of ways, Harry Ramsden was the proudest of Yorkshiremen.

Punctuality was a fetish with him. It was not merely the politeness of princes.

If young Harry was driving him to an appointment he insisted on leaving at least half an hour before he was due to be in Leeds, or Bradford, even if he had to hang about when he reached his destination. At the appointed time, only then would he go into the office of the solicitor, the accountant or business associate he had gone to see. "Son," he told young Harry (and it has remained with the younger man all his life), "the appointment is for three o'clock – not five to, or five past, but three o'clock. That's the time I shall be there."

The development of his business instincts and principles was a gradual process. Perhaps it began in Blackpool when he was twelve years old when he got the better of one of those fast-talking Dutch auctioneers on the Golden Mile. It most certainly developed from his experience with one of the cab-cleaners during his days with the Northern Motor Cab Company Ltd., one Fred Brook, who announced to Harry that he had found a gold sovereign in one of the cars.

"I don't know what to do about it," he confessed.

"I should keep it," advised Harry, "if no one has come back to claim it."

"That's all reight, then," said the delighted Mr. Brook, "Cos it were in your cab that I found it."

Harry "got on" with a wide spectrum of acquaintances – the rich and famous and the poor and needy alike. Perhaps his most remarkable relationship was with Jimmy Jackson, the teenager who walked from London in 1923 to stay with his brother and to work at an engineering plant in Horbury. He left his digs "because he didn't get on with his sister-in-law" and he quit the job after "a bit of a scrap with a feller there". Not, it seems, the easiest sort of person to get along with. But it was while he was doing a bit of work as a gardener at the Blighty (British Legion) Club in Bradford that he met Harry Ramsden, one of the members. He was invited to the Bower Street shop to do some washing up on Saturday nights, "graduated" to fryer and moved with Harry to White Cross in 1928, remaining with him until the mid-1950s. But in between he experienced the essential kindness and generosity of the fish-and-chip king. After taking him on as a casual assistant, Harry took Jimmy to Gaunt's gents' outfitters in Bradford and bought him "two of everything".

"He then told me to go to the Windsor Baths and get myself cleaned up," recalls Jimmy, "and he took me home with him to live at Southbrook Terrace" with its colourful population of theatricals, footballers and the girls from County Durham. And here perhaps we may digress for a moment to recall a bit of newspaper history.

64

Gilbert Harding enjoying some of the White Cross fish-and-chips.

The *Telegraph and Argus* at the time had a small Saturday column in its sports paper, the pink Star Final, called "Tops and Noils" in which were printed jokes, not always of the highest quality but they suited the mood of 1920s readership. The Telegraph paid 10 shillings for the best tale, five bob for the second-best and half-a-crown for the third and it was at least worth the price of a 1½d stamp to have a go. (My own memory lingers fondly on Tops and Noils because there was a man in the village of Eastburn, where I was brought up, who regularly supplemented his income in this way and thus was much envied by the lads of the village – H. Eccles was his name.)

So it was a delight to find Jimmy Jackson, a Bradford City supporter, recalling one of these witticisms, more than 50 years after it appeared in the *Telegraph*. City had a player called Moon at that time and Jimmy was asked by an acquaintance, "What were t'match like last neet?" "Not bad," he replied non-committally. "Well," said his friend, "it should have been all reight – Moon were out." And he enjoyed the exchange so much he sent off the quote to "t'Sports" and was duly rewarded.

Jimmy stayed at White Cross until the mid-fifties when ill-health and the pressure of running the world's greatest fish and chip shop were beginning to tell on Harry. His business had survived the Second World War which created, of course, problems for all caterers. It was difficult to get supplies of fish – sometimes his ration was as little as five pounds a day so it had to be carefully chopped and shredded and made into fish-cakes. A few tins of low-grade salmon could be made into salmon fish-cakes but his staple meal became *egg* and chips. Ministry of Food inspectors, whose job it was to make sure that the black market did not flourish (or to limit it as much as possible!), were eagle-eyed and industrious but not, happily, without a sense of humour. One, paying a periodic call at White Cross, noted a modest dozen hens which Harry kept at the back of the restaurant and related it to the number of egg-and-chip meals which had been served. "Them poor little buggers must 'av reight sore backsides," he reflected, but pursued the matter no further. Harry Ramsden's was an institution which was providing a public service. It is not stretching the point too far by any means to reflect that it must been a contribution to wartime morale to see the business still operating, even if it was shorn of its illuminated sign and the fairy lights twinkling in the tree outside the entrance. A black-out there might be; austerity engulfed us on all sides, but "Harry's" was still open for business.

Food rationing continued for nine years after the war, it should be remembered. The United Nations Organisation had been formed, the coal mines and the railways nationalised and the National Health Service instituted. King George VI had died and his daughter had been crowned Queen Elizabeth II; floods had twice ravaged the British east coast, Stalin had died and strife-torn Vietnam was still called French Indo-China when the last rationing regulation in Britain ended in July, 1954.

Harry Ramsden's fish-and-chip restaurant had lived through stirring times. And as prices began to rise Harry began to have serious doubts. "Fish is going to cost fourpence," he pondered, sadly, "and folk'll nivver pay it. They won't." And he began to get "Closing down" signs ready for display in the shop and restaurant.

"Nay, Harry," said a friend, "give 'em a chance. Wait to see if they *will* pay afore tha shuts up shop." He did, and they did, but it still worried Harry. More and more he began to yearn to get away from the constant ringing of the telephone, the incessant calls upon him for decisions, the problems of handling an ever-growing army of staff. More and more he longed to get away from it all and enjoy those long walks over the edge of the moors and to leave the cares of business for the escapism of his love of the countryside and his pride in being a Yorkshireman. Visionary that he was in so many ways, even Harry Ramsden could not foresee the day when a humble haddock fillet would cost over a pound and a penn'orth of chips would go up to the equivalent of five bob or more. If anyone had told him it would happen, he wouldn't have believed it.

The strain was becoming too much. In 1954 a new company was formed called Ramsden (White Cross) Ltd., with Harry still a director and John Edward (Eddie) Stokes as managing director. Mr. Stokes was experienced in the catering trade in Blackpool and his contract gave him the option to buy the business if he wished, at a later date. The way was clear for Harry to start to enjoy a life of at least semi-retirement with the running of White Cross in Eddie Stokes' hands. Did he do so...?

Within months he had started a new fish-and-chip shop in Shipley, opened with due ceremony, by Sooty – who else! Cousin Sooty. And this was followed by a second shop in the Horsefair at Wetherby. By now Harry was a sick man and cancer had been diagnosed. He spent months in the Duke of York's Nursing Home in Bradford but refused an operation which might, or might not, have helped him. It seems tragically true that in establishing the world's greatest fish-and-chip shop he had created a sort of Frankenstein's monster which had

The Harry Ramsden touch. On his semi-retirement, he transformed Windsor Fisheries at Shipley (*left*) into a smart little shop (*below*).

become too big for him to control and yet he could not leave the trade alone. The lather-boy, millhand, taxi-driver and publican had found his real vocation and if he could not abandon it completely who is to say he was wrong? He was a unique character and he had built a unique business, one which was known to people in the farthest corners of the world. There was only one Harry Ramsden's and he was the man who made it.

He died on January 7th, 1963 in Middleton Hospital, Ilkley, and Guiseley Parish Church was filled for a service of remembrance the following week. Harry had willed his body to Leeds University School of Medicine for research so it was not until two years later that his remains were finally laid to rest in the church's Garden of Remembrance. The *Telegraph and Argus* headline provided the perfect epitaph: "Goodbye, Mr. Chips".

Harry stood at the Pearly Gate,
His face was worn and old,
He meekly asked the man of fate,
Admission to the fold,
"What have you done" old Peter asked,
"-to seek admittance here "?
I owned a Guiseley Fish Shop
For many & many a year,
The gate flew open sharply, as
Peter touched the bell,
"Come in old man, & take a harp,
You've had enough - of Hell..

Epilogue

EDDIE Stokes took up his option and bought the business for £37,500 in 1954, selling it in August 1965 to the Essex-based Associated Fisheries (Restaurants) Ltd.

Associated Fisheries continued the Harry Ramsden tradition until April, 1988, when the restaurant was acquired by the present management team. Their commitment to Harry Ramsden's legacy of quality and high standards of presentation has been maintained and when the Diamond Jubilee of Harry's first move to White Cross was celebrated in October, 1988, it was in similar style to Harry's festivities to mark his Silver Jubilee. At the end of week-long partying (clowns, jugglers, magicians, TV and stage personalities) fish and chips were once again served for twopence a portion and it was all rounded off with a firework display. The editor of the Guinness Book of Records (which features Harry's as the world's largest fish and chip shop) was there to record another landmark — the highest number of people served in one day: 10,182 of them who demolished 183 stones of fish and 5,500 lbs of potatoes, all fried in 1,692 lbs of dripping. And this record was, in turn, overtaken when the now internationally-expanding firm opened a restaurant in Glasgow on 17 May 1992, and served 11,964 customers. The Scots have never been slow to recognise a bargain when they see it.

In November, 1989 Harry Ramsden's shares were floated on the London Stock Exchange and a future policy of expansion was announced of opening more Harry Ramsden's restaurants modelled on the original in Guiseley. The share-issue was over-subscribed 2.8 times.

In 1990 the first of the new Harry Ramsden's restaurants was opened in Blackpool; the following year came the record-breaking opening of the Glasgow restaurant. Next came Hong Kong (August, 1992), the first international venture, and two years after that my friend Freddie Trueman flew out to launch the serving of Theakston's bitter beer in that restaurant. What will Communist China make of that when they take over Hong Kong in 1997?

By the middle of 1994 Harry Ramsden's had 11 restaurants in the UK and one in Hong Kong. Future plans involved another ten restaurants in the UK and further international expansion in Australia, Singapore and the Middle East.

What would old Harry have thought of it? There can be little doubt that he would have swelled with pride. He would, certainly, have approved. He had envied his son the massive changes "young" Harry was going to experience in his lifetime and, as we have seen, the maestro firmly believed that in business you can never stand still. Oh yes — uncrowned he might have been but of his kingship there can be no doubt.

I can think of only one thing which might have upset him — as a good patriot and cricket-lover. On Monday, 12th June, 1989, the management invited the whole Australian cricket tour party for dinner at Guiseley during the First Test at Headingley. With one day's play remaining England had no chance of winning but they were in a perfectly reasonable position to save the match. That evening the Australians celebrated Terry Alderman's 32nd birthday. The following morning Terry went out at Headingley and bowled Australia to victory by 210 runs. Now Harry wouldn't have liked that overmuch.

Above all he was a cricket-loving Yorkshireman and thus deeply emotional about such matters. Yet I wouldn't mind betting that he would have somehow turned it to his advantage. Can't you just see the final message on Headingley's electronic scoreboard as the players left the field: "Harry Ramsden's fish and chips have passed the Test"?

Sincere thanks...

WITHOUT the hard work and loyalty of the full supporting cast of Harry Ramsden's, this book would not have been written. My sincere thanks to them all (and to any names I may have inadvertently omitted):–

Will Adamson; Dorothy Beer; Ernest Beer; Clifford and Derek Berry; Harold Britton; Shirley Britton; Fred Brooke; Audrey Brooks; Florrie Broughton; Harriet Broughton; Al Brown; Joyce, Marion & Nancy Claughton; Violet Clegg; Jim Cole; Marjorie Corbett; Maureen Cowling; Mr. Croft; Frank Crook; June Daniels; Gerald Dawson; Bert & Flo Dennis; Lena Dennison; Dorothy Doubtfire; Mary Downs; Vera Dunne; Anne Ewell; Alice Farrar; Mr. & Mrs. Forest; Ida Glover; Nellie Gore; May Greenwood; Horace Harbron; Mabel Harrison; Arthur Hooper; Mr. & Mrs. Hooper; Mrs. Ineson; Alec Jackson; Jim Jackson; Kath Jackson; May Jackson; Stan Jackson; Peggy Jones; Mary Lee; Dennis Light; Maureen McCaig; Horace Nelson; Bert & Joan Nesbit; Ivor Oakley; Eva, Jean & Mary Ormston; Mary Outing; Irene Poucher; Kathleen Pullan; Mary Rathmell; Jean Robinson; Mr. & Mrs. Robinson; Jimmy Roebuck; Irene, Jesse, Lilian & Muriel Sharp; Ivy Sharp; Sylvia Short; Mary Sloane; Sally Smith; Harry Sugden; Jean Todd; Jimmy Trotter; Harold & May Walker; Tommy Walker; Edith Walsh; Rita Walsh; Alice Wildsmith; Carol Windas; Elsie Windas; Arthur Wood; Eric Wood.

– Harry Ramsden Junior

Harry Ramsden Junior – in 1940.